J.S. BACH

A Little Keyboard Book
of 39 pieces

Edited and annotated by

RICHARD JONES

THE ASSOCIATED BOARD OF
THE ROYAL SCHOOLS OF MUSIC

For
Rowan Paul Jones
and
Samuel George Barrows

INTRODUCTION

This volume is intended as a first book of Bach for the keyboard player. As such it might be employed as a preliminary to the series: Inventions & Sinfonias, French Suites, English Suites, Partitas, and *The Well-Tempered Clavier* I & II. There is documentary evidence that this series in general corresponds to the order in which Bach taught his own keyboard music. But, in addition, there is good reason to suppose that he might have regarded 'A Little Keyboard Book' as a suitable introduction to the series. The title of the book and most of its contents are reproduced from Bach's *Clavierbüchlein* of 1720, the little manuscript book which he devoted to the instruction in keyboard playing and composition of his eldest son, Wilhelm Friedemann, then only nine years old. It was Bach's habit to teach his pupils compositions originally written for the instruction and delectation of members of his own family. And it is in this spirit that the present publication has been devised.

As a historical document the *Clavierbüchlein* for Wilhelm Friedemann Bach has been well-served since 1950: by the publication, first, of Ralph Kirkpatrick's facsimile edition (New Haven, 1959) and, shortly thereafter, of Wolfgang Plath's edition for the Neue Bach-Ausgabe (Series V, Vol. 5; Kassel & Leipzig, 1962). The present Associated Board edition aims, above all, at rendering it practicable as a first Bach book for the modern player. With this in mind, the early versions in the *Clavierbüchlein* of eleven Preludes from *The Well-Tempered Clavier* (Book I) and of the Inventions & Sinfonias have been omitted: these pieces belong to later stages in the Bach player's development and most people will, in any case, want to play Bach's later, definitive versions. Balancing, as it happens, the loss of the Preludes from the '48', eleven shorter and easier Preludes (BWV 933-43), drawn from other sources, have been included. These form a natural complement to the short Preludes of the *Clavierbüchlein* (BWV 924-8, 930 & 932), for in both cases Bach's intention was clearly to provide keyboard studies and composition models or exercises at an elementary stage.

Three further effects of the present editor's practical aim should be noticed. Firstly, he has undertaken the task of completing the five pieces (BWV 753, 837 & 932; J.C. Richter: Allemande & Courante) that survive only as fragments. As a result they are no longer mere historical curiosities but can be brought to life as significant additions to the modern player's repertoire. Secondly, the editor has placed the pieces from the *Clavierbüchlein* in a slightly different, somewhat more rational order. This represents very much the sort of re-ordering that Bach himself might have carried out had he contemplated publication. Thirdly, editorial assistance is offered in the form of tempo markings (in square brackets), fingering, suggestions for the execution of, or for additional, ornaments (between the staves; small print or square brackets), punctuation of phrasing (commas, bracketed commas for subdivisions), staccato (square brackets), legato (⌒),

legatissimo & tenuto (notation between the staves), and additional inner parts where necessary (small print). These editorial markings are, in every case, intended to encourage stylish playing, but it would be mistaken to follow them slavishly or to regard them with undue reverence. Other solutions to the problems of interpretation which arise here may be perfectly valid, and what has to be acquired above all is the taste or sense of style which would enable the player successfully to follow his own inclinations.

It ought to be pointed out to the teacher that 'A Little Keyboard Book' is not suitable for beginners. The very first piece in the book, the Applicatio, is – as Plath rightly judges (op. cit.) – too difficult for the novice, even for one as musically gifted as Wilhelm Friedemann Bach. As a form of preparation for the book, the mostly anonymous little pieces in the *Clavierbüchlein* for Anna Magdalena Bach of 1725 provide an obvious choice.

Finally, a word about the order of study. It is not intended that the order of the pieces in this book should correspond to the order in which they are studied. A better approach would be to divide the contents into three classes: the preludes, together with the single fugue (which, from a didactic point of view, belongs with the more strictly contrapuntal preludes); the dances and suites; and the elaborately ornamented pieces. The three types might be studied concurrently. Within them a suitable order of study might be roughly as follows:

Preludes, Fugue	*Dances, Suites*	*Ornamented Pieces*
4 Preludes, BWV 939-42	3 Minuets	Applicatio
3 Preludes, BWV 924a, 925, 932	2 Allemandes	2 Chorale Preludes
5 Preludes, BWV 924, 926-8, 930	Richter	Prelude in A minor,
6 Preludes, BWV 933-8	Stölzel	BWV 931
Prelude in C, BWV 943	Telemann	
Fugue in C, BWV 953		

The largely two-part Preludes prepare for the Inventions; the three-part ones (especially BWV 943) for the Sinfonias. After working through the dances and suites, the player might be able to tackle the easier dances in the French and English Suites. The Applicatio offers a useful study in executing ornaments; the chorale preludes provide an introduction to Bach's florid style and – for organists – to the organ chorale; and the A minor Prelude (anonymous despite its BWV number) gives a foretaste of the ornamental style of the French *clavecinistes*. The presence of this and other pieces not composed by Bach allows the book to serve as an introduction not only to his keyboard music but to early 18th-century keyboard style in general.

Thanks are due to the Musikabteilung of the Staatsbibliothek Preussischer Kulturbesitz, Berlin for providing mircofilms and for permitting their use as sources.

RICHARD JONES
Oxford, 1985

CONTENTS

From the *Clavierbüchlein* for W. F. Bach

Applicatio in C, BWV 994 — Page 8

Five Preludes
No. 1 in C, BWV 924 — 8
No. 2 in D Minor, BWV 926 — 10
No. 3 in F, BWV 927 — 12
No. 4 in G minor, BWV 930 — 13
No. 5 in F, BWV 928 — 14

Two Allemandes
No. 1 in G minor, BWV 836 — 16
No. 2 in G minor, BWV 837 — 17

Three Minuets
No. 1 in G, BWV 841 — 18
No. 2 in G minor, BWV 842 — 18
No. 3 in G, BWV 843 — 19

Two Choral Preludes
Wer nur den lieben Gott, BWV 691 — Page 20
Jesu meine Freude, BWV 753 — 21

Three Preludes
No. 1 in C, BWV 924a — 22
No. 2 in D, BWV 925 — 23
No. 3 in E minor, BWV 932 — 24

Prelude in A minor, BWV 931 — 25

Fugue in C, BWV 953 — 26

J. C. Richter: Allemande & Courante
Allemande — 28
Courante — 30

From the *Clavierbüchlein* for W.F.Bach

G.P.Telemann: Suite in A

1. Allemande

Page
32

2. Courante

34

3. Gigue

36

G.H.Stölzel: Partita in G minor

1. Overture

39

2. Air Italien

42

3. Bourrée

43

4. Minuet

44

5. Minuet-Trio (J.S.Bach, BWV 929)

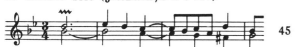
45

Other pieces

Four Preludes

No.1 in C, BWV 939

Page
46

No.2 in D minor, BWV 940

47

No.3 in E minor, BWV 941

48

No.4 in A minor, BWV 942

49

Prelude in C, BWV 943

50

Six Preludes

No.1 in C, BWV 933

52

No.2 in C minor, BWV 934

53

No.3 in D minor, BWV 935

54

No.4 in D, BWV 936

56

No.5 in E, BWV 937

58

No.6 in E minor, BWV 938

60

TABLE OF ORNAMENTS

Explication unterschiedlicher Zeichen, so gewisse *manieren* artig zu spielen, andeuten

Explanation of various signs showing how to play certain ornaments neatly

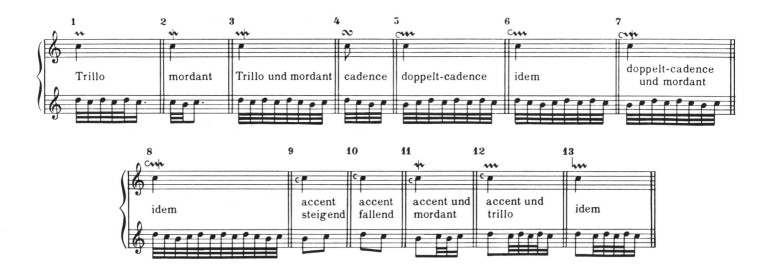

1. Shake.   It may be shortened to: ![symbol] ; for the longer form, the sign ⁓ is sometimes used. Both ⁓ and ⁓ are interchangeable with *tr.* In practice the length of the shake will depend on the length of the note to which it applies. Shakes occasionally begin on the main note, depending on context.

2. Mordent.   It may sometimes be lengthened to ![symbol]

3. Long shake with closing notes.   The sign is interchangeable with *tr.*

4. Turn.   When placed *between* two notes – ![symbol] – it should be executed thus: ![symbol]

5. Shake with rising prefix.

6. Shake with falling prefix.

7. Shake with rising prefix and closing notes.

8. Shake with falling prefix and closing notes.

9. Rising appoggiatura and 10. Falling appoggiatura.
   The sign is interchangeable with ![symbol]. The length of the ornament depends on context, ranging from ![symbol] to ![symbol]. When filling the interval of a falling third – ![symbol] – the ornament sometimes anticipates the beat, thus: ![symbol].

11. Rising appoggiatura with mordent.

12. Falling appoggiatura with shake.

13. The same as no. 12.

APPLICATIO in C
BWV 994

As its name implies, this piece is a practical application of what has been learnt about ornaments in the Explication. Like the Prelude in G minor, BWV 930, it is fully fingered by Bach himself. In this edition Bach's fingering is given in normal type; the editor's fingering in italics.

FIVE PRELUDES
No. 1 in C
BWV 924

AB 1965

The pedal bass in bb.11-17 will need to be re-struck at least once. The shake in b.15 is best begun on the main note, thus: ♪♪♪♪ . For an alternative version of this piece, see BWV 924a (p.22).

No. 2 in D minor
BWV 926

The cadenza-like passage in bb.39-42 can be handled freely (upstems here denote R.H., downstems L.H.). The *ossia* in b.43, which has the effect of extending the cadenza for one more bar, is Bach's own.

AB 1965

No. 3 in F
BWV 927

No. 4 in G minor
BWV 930

The fingering in normal type is Bach's own; that in italics, editorial. The R.H. and L.H. mordents in b.39 are best regarded as alternatives.

AB 1965

No. 5 in F
BWV 928

TWO ALLEMANDES
No.1 in G minor

Both this Allemande and the one that follows were probably composed by the young Wilhelm Friedemann Bach with his father's help. The tripartite structure of No.1 may be intentional, but it is more likely that the third section (following the second double bar) is a correction of the second (upbeat to b.6 – b.12). This middle section has been included here for interest's sake, but it is probably best to play only sections 1 and 3.

Part of b.4 is missing in the manuscript due to careless copying on Friedemann's part; it has been completed here by the editor. The final phrase – bb.17-20 – is in Johann Sebastian's hand and may have been composed by him.

AB 1965

No. 2 in G minor

Probably by Wilhelm Friedemann, perhaps with his father's help. The composition breaks off halfway through b.8 (a leaf is missing in the manuscript at this point) and has been completed by the editor.

THREE MINUETS
No. 1 in G
BWV 841

No. 2 in G minor
BWV 842

No. 3 in G
BWV 843

TWO CHORALE PRELUDES
Wer nur den lieben Gott lässt walten
BWV 691

The plain chorale melody which precedes the elaborated version is borrowed, for the purposes of this edition, from the last movement of the Cantata, 'Siehe zu, dass deine Gottesfurcht nicht Heuchelei sei', BWV 179.

AB 1965

Jesu, meine Freude
BWV 753

The plain chorale melody which precedes the elaborated version is borrowed from the last movement of the Cantata, 'Bisher habt ihr nichts gebeten in meinem Namen', BWV 87. The Chorale Prelude breaks off after the 3rd crotchet of b.9: it was apparently left unfinished by Bach. The last 4 bb. (plus one crotchet) are composed by the editor.

THREE PRELUDES
No. 1 in C
BWV 924a

This Prelude – a re-working of the Prelude in C, BWV 924 (see p.8) – and the two that follow are probably composition exercises of Wilhelm Friedemann Bach's (by then, perhaps, in his mid-teens), no doubt supervised or assisted by his father.

No. 2 in D
BWV 925

[Moderato]

No. 3 in E minor
BWV 932

This piece breaks off after the 1st crotchet of b.11 and may have been left unfinished, for the next page in the manuscript is blank. It has been completed by the editor.

Prelude in A minor

Anon.

1) or

This piece is in the style of the French *clavecinistes* and may in fact – as Walter Emery suggested – have been written by a Frenchman; it is certainly not by Bach.

AB 1965

FUGUE in C
BWV 953

ALLEMANDE

J. C. Richter

COURANTE

J. C. Richter (?)

Wilhelm Friedemann Bach left his copies of both the Allemande and the Courante unfinished in the manuscript due to lack of space at the end of a page. The endings given here (within square brackets) are composed by the editor.

AB 1965

SUITE in A

G. P. Telemann

1. Allemande

2. Courante

3. Gigue

38

PARTITA in G minor

G. H. Stölzel

1. Overture
[Grave]

AB 1965

2. Air Italien
[Andante]

3. Bourrée

Bars 11-12 appear to have been miscopied by Wilhelm Friedemann and have been reconstructed here by the editor.

4. Minuet

5. Minuet - Trio, BWV 929

J. S. Bach

[No. 4 Minuet D.C.]

The first-time bar in No.4 (b.32a) is editorial. No.5 is a composition of Johann Sebastian's which he himself added as a Trio to Stölzel's Minuet.

AB 1965

FOUR PRELUDES
No. 1 in C
BWV 939

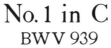

No. 2 in D minor
BWV 940

No. 3 in E minor
BWV 941

No. 4 in A minor
BWV 942

[Allegro]

The L.H. part of b.9 is editorial (the writer of the MS accidentally copied out the bass of the previous bar here a second time).

AB 1965

PRELUDE in C
BWV 943

The sign ⌐‾⌐ signifies hemiola rhythm. The tonic pedal in bb.53 ff. will need to be re-struck at least once.

AB 1965

SIX PRELUDES
No. 1 in C major
BWV 933

No. 2 in C minor
BWV 934

No. 3 in D minor

BWV 935

No. 4 in D major
BWV 936

Suggested phrasing of the theme:

No. 5 in E major
BWV 937

This piece is, like many of the Inventions, constructed almost entirely in double counterpoint.

No. 6 in E minor
BWV 938

The source of all but the last eleven pieces in this volume is the *Clavierbüchlein* for Wilhelm Friedemann Bach (original in the Library of the School of Music, Yale University, New Haven, Connecticut, U.S.A.; facsimile edition, ed. R. Kirkpatrick, Yale University Press, New Haven, 1959). The title of this small oblong MS book reads:

Clavier-Büchlein./vor/Wilhelm Friedemann Bach./angefangen in/Cöthen den/22. Januarii/Ao. 1720.

The contents are almost exclusively in either Johann Sebastian's or Wilhelm Friedemann Bach's hand (it is not always easy to distinguish between the two, and the handwriting attributions given below are indebted to the research of Wolfgang Plath as published in the *Kritischer Bericht* to NBA V/5). In the brief commentary which follows, the 'Cb' number discloses the order of the pieces within the *Clavierbüchlein*. This does not entirely correspond to their chronological order. Plath's conclusions over chronology may be summarized as follows:

Cb 1-24 (except No.8): 1720 – c. 1722
Cb 32-62 (plus No.8, 1st half): late 1722 – early 1723
Cb 25-31 (plus No.8, 2nd half): 1724-6

Cb – Explication (Table of Ornaments). Hand: J.S.B. Preceded by 'Claves signatae', also autograph: a table showing the clef signs and the names of the notes (omitted from the present edition).

Cb 1 Applicatio in C, BWV 994. Autograph.

Cb 2 Prelude No.1 in C, BWV 924. Autograph. Title: Praeambulum 1. The keys of the first two Preludes – C and d – coupled with their autograph numbering as 1 and 2, suggest that Bach may originally have planned a set in an ascending key series, alternating major and minor modes; thus: C d E f G a.

Cb 4 Prelude No.2 in D minor, BWV 926. Autograph. Title: Praeludium 2. The intended duration of Bach's slurs in bb.9-10 & 13-14 is unclear; perhaps they should start from the beginning of bb.9 & 13.

Cb 8 Prelude No.3 in F, BWV 927. In W.F. Bach's hand. Title: Praeambulum.

Cb 9 Prelude No.4 in G minor, BWV 930. Autograph. Title: Praeambulum. Key signature: one flat.

Cb 10 Prelude No.5 in F, BWV 928. Autograph. Title: Praeludium.

Cb 6 Allemande No.1 in G minor, BWV 836. Hand: W.F.B. and J.S.B. Title: Allemande. Composer: probably W.F. Bach, perhaps with his father's assistance. Key signature: one flat.

Cb 7 Allemande No.2 in G minor, BWV 837. Hand: W.F.B., J.S.B. & anon. Title: Allemande. Composer: probably W.F. Bach, perhaps with his father's assistance. Key signature: one flat. Bar 6, R.H., 4th crotchet: equal quavers; b.4, 6th bass note: *f*, not *d*, in error.

Three Minuets, BWV 841-3. These pieces were clearly designed as a triptych: they are numbered 1-3, form the key-series G g G, and share the figure ♪♫ .

Cb 11 Minuet No.1 in G, BWV 841. In W.F. Bach's hand. Title: Menuet 1. The composition may not be entirely Bach's: it is possible that he added a bass to a pre-existing melody. The piece is pre-

sent also in the *Clavierbüchlein* for Anna Magdalena Bach of 1722 (No.11, p.50; probably in A.M.B.'s hand; copy from Cb or its source; text virtually identical).

Cb 12 Minuet No.2 in G minor, BWV 842. Hand: W.F.B. and J.S.B. Title: Menuet 2. Time signature: 3. Bar 14, R.H.: ♪♪♪♪♪♪ in error (cf. b.6).

Cb 13 Minuet No.3 in G, BWV 843. Autograph. Title: Menuet 3. Time signature: 3. According to Plath, possibly transposed down from C major. Bar 24, 5th bass note: *B*; corr. by the editor to *A*.

Cb 3 Wer nur den lieben Gott lässt walten, BWV 691. Autograph. A copy in Anna Magdalena's hand is present in her *Clavierbüchlein* of 1725 (No.11, p.55; text identical, except that A.M.B. gives fewer ornaments).

Cb 5 Jesu meine Freude, BWV 753. Autograph.

[Cb 14-24] Early versions of eleven Preludes from *The Well-Tempered Clavier* (Book 1). Not included in this edition.

Three Preludes, BWV 924a, 925 and 932. In W.F. Bach's hand. All three are probably composition exercises of W.F. Bach's, perhaps supervised or assisted by his father. No.1 is closely modelled on the C major Prelude, BWV 924. This fact, in conjunction with the uniform titles (see below) and the tonal scheme – C D e – suggests that Friedemann planned a series of preludes analogous to the set begun by his father (see above under BWV 924).

Cb 26 Prelude No.1 in C, BWV 924a. Title: Praeludium ex c♮.

Cb 27 Prelude No.2 in D, BWV 925. Title: Praeludium ex d♮. Pause to 1st bass & treble note of b.15; perhaps the piece originally terminated at this point.

Cb 28 Prelude No.3 in E minor, BWV 932. Title: Praeludium ex e♮. Bar 2, 1st treble note: *e'*; corr. to *g'* by the editor; b.9, 4th crotchet, bass *a*: sharp; corr. to natural by the editor; b.11, 1st crotchet: crotchet *d'* editorial.

Cb 29 Prelude in A minor, BWV 931. In W.F. Bach's hand. Title: Praeludium. Composer: anon. Bars 6-7, R.H.: falling appoggiaturas, presumably in error; as the late Walter Emery pointed out (*Bach's Ornaments*, London, 1953, p.123), the context requires rising appoggiaturas.

[Cb 30] Anon. bass sketch in G minor. Hand: anon. Not included in this edition.

Cb 31 Fugue in C, BWV 953. Autograph (possibly 1st draft). Title: Fuga à 3.

Cb 25 J.C. Richter: Allemande and Courante.

Allemande . In W.F. Bach's hand. Title: Pièce pour le Clavecin, composée par J.C. Richter[;] Allemande. The composer is probably one of the two Richters who were employed in Dresden: the oboist, Johann Christian Richter (1689-1744); or the court organist, Johann Christoph Richter (1700-1785). Bar 17, alto, 1st half-bar: four *a*'s, not *g*'s, in error; b.20, R.H., 3rd crotchet: identical with 1st crotchet, but cf. bb.4-5.

Courante. In W.F. Bach's hand. Title: Courante. Composer: J.C. Richter? (Or composition exercise of W.F.B.'s?). Bar 3, 1st treble note: *c''*, not *d''*, in error; 5th treble note: *a'*, not *b'*, in error; b.22: dotted minim chord; b.29, 2nd bass note: *e'*, not *d'*, in error; b.30: 2nd bass note double-stemmed; b.37, bass, 3rd crotchet: [musical symbols]

[Cb 32-46] Original versions of the fifteen two-part Inventions, BWV 772-786. Not included in this edition.

Cb 47 G.P. Telemann (1681-1767): Suite in A (erroneously included in Schmieder's Bach catalogue as BWV 824). In W.F. Bach's hand.

1. Allemande (thus entitled). W.F.B. included three additional mordents (at b.4, 5th treble note; b.5, 1st bass note; and b.11, last treble note) but later crossed them out. The 7th note of the opening 8-note figure is notated inconsistently – 1st half of b.10: *e″*, not *b′* (but *b′* in the two following half-bars); bb.29-30: *a″*, not *e″*.

2. Courante (thus entitled). Bar 19, alto, 3rd crotchet: *g′* sharp; corr. by the editor to *a′*.

3. Gigue (thus entitled). Bars 8 & 16 are inconsistent but have been left unaltered in this edition; b.21, L.H. and all parallel bars read: | ♩ ▬ | ; the *c′* sharp in the 1st chord of b.28 is an editorial correction : the source reads *b*; and in b.39 the mordents apply to the alto, not the treble, but this must be an error.

Cb 48 G.H. Stölzel (1690-1749): Partita in G minor. Movements 1-4 in W.F. Bach's hand; 5th movement: autograph of a Minuet by J.S. Bach, added as Trio to Stölzel's Minuet (4th movement). Title: Partia di Signore Steltzeln.

1. Overture. Title: Ouverture. The appoggiaturas in bb.19 ff. are signified by small slurs, not by hooks. The slurs in bb.59ff. are short and may apply only to the first two notes in each case. Bars 20 and 48 are inconsistent, but neither has been altered in this edition.

2. Air Italien (thus entitled). Bar 8: superfluous quaver rests in all parts before the double-bar; b.17, last quaver, *d″*: editorial correction; W.F.B has *f″* (no sharp); b.23, 2nd bass note: ? originally *a* flat, corr. to *f*.

3. Bourrée (thus entitled). Bar 11, R.H. and b.12, L.H. are missing due to a copying error of W.F.B's and have been reconstructed by the editor. The alto part in bb.18-19 is a tone too high (*g′ a′*, *f′ g′*). 3rd treble note of b.18: *f″*, not *e″* flat, in error.

4. Minuet. Title: Menuet. In b.17, L.H., crotchets 1-2, two crotchet *d*'s are separated by a line-change; presumably they should be tied. Bar 28, R.H.: dotted crotchet *g″*. The 1st-time bar, b.32a, is editorial.

5. Minuet-Trio. Title: Menuet-Trio di JS Bach. Probably 1st draft.

[Cb 49-62] Original versions of fourteen of the fifteen three-part Sinfonias (the last is missing), BWV 787-801. Not included in this edition.

Four Preludes, BWV 939-42. The source of these pieces – their sole surviving source – is Fascicle 53 (pp.373-6) of Mus. Ms. Bach P804, Berlin, Staatsbibliothek Preussischer Kulturbesitz, Musikabteilung. P804 contains 57 originally independent MSS, most of which are in the hand of Johann Peter Kellner (1705-1772). The contents of Fascicle 53 are as follows:
   p.373: blank
   p.374: BWV 940, 941, 939
   p.375: BWV 927, 942
   p.376: blank
Both general and individual titles are lacking. The handwriting is possibly an early form of Kellner's. The probable date is some time between 1725 and 1750.

These four Preludes, together with the Prelude in C minor, BWV 999 and seven pieces from the *Clavierbüchlein* for W.F.B. (BWV 924-30) have become widely known as the 'Zwölf kleine Praeludien' (Twelve Little Preludes) ever since they were published as such by F.C Griepenkerl in the mid-19th century. In the present Associated Board edition, the *Clavierbüchlein* pieces are, of course, placed within their authentic context, and the C minor Prelude is omitted: in its sole source – Fascicle 19 (pp.101-4) of P804 – it is clearly designated by Kellner 'Praelude pour la lute'.

No.1 in C, BWV 939. The uncharacteristic and inferior writing in bb.6 & 15 raises the question whether we have here – and, by extension, in the other Preludes of this group (BWV 940-2) – a composition exercise supervised or assisted by Bach (cf. BWV 924a, 925 & 932 from the *Clavierbüchlein* for W.F.B) rather than an original composition of Bach's own. There are two obvious errors in the bass – 1st L.H. note of b.6: *b*; last of b.13: *g*.

No.2 in D minor, BWV 940. Key signature: no flat. 2nd alto note of b.5: mordent, not shake; 2nd half of b.7, tenor: ♩ ♫ (sic).

No.3 in E minor, BWV 941. 2nd bass note of b.8: *a*, not *g*; 3rd treble note of b.10: mordent, not shake; 1st crochet of b.21, treble: ♫♩ .

No.4 in A minor, BWV 942. Bar 9, L.H. is missing due to a copying error (the L.H. of b.8 was copied out again in b.9).

Prelude in C, BWV 943. Source: Fascicle 2 (pp.5-8) of Mus. ms. Bach P804 (see above under BWV 939-42). The copy occupies pp.6-7 of the MS (p.5: title; p.8: blank) and is in J.P. Kellner's hand. The title reads: Praeludium in C♮/di/Johann Sebastian Bach. In the bottom R.H. corner of the title-page is the signature: Poss./Johann Peter Kellner. It is unclear whether the 1st alto note of b.42 is *e′* or *f′*. The tenor quavers in b.45 are notated a tone too high (*g a b*). And the L.H. minims in the final bar are dotted.

Six Preludes, BWV 933-8. The sources, all from Berlin, Staatsbibliothek Preussischer Kulturbesitz, Musikabteilung, are as follows:

A   Mus. ms. Bach P528. 8pp.(pp.1 & 8 blank).
   Contents: BWV 933-8 in the order 938, 933-5, 937, 936.
   Hand: anon., 2nd half of the 18th century.
B   Mus. ms. Bach P540. 8pp. (p.1: title; p.8: blank).
   Contents: BWV 933-8 in that order.
   Title: Six Preludes à l'usage des Commençants/composès/par/ Jean Sebastian Bach.
   Hand: J.N. Forkel (1749-1818).
C   Mus. ms. Bach P542. 46pp.
   Contents: BWV 772-801, 961, 933-8 (in that order; pp.32-7), 906, and 819.
   Hand: anon. copyist employed by the owner whose signature appears on the title- page: Graf Karl Lichnowsky, Göttingen 1781.
D   Mus. ms. Bach P672. 84pp.
   Contents: include (on pp.8-15) BWV 933, 934, 937 and 938 (numbered 1-4).
   Title: ·Kleine Clavier=Stücke./von/J.S. Bach./C.P.E. Bach./ J.C. Bach. /J.C.F. Bach./Altnickol.
   Hand: Michel (Hamburg copyist of C.P.E. Bach's).
   Date: probably 1780s.

E   Mus. ms. Bach P885. 6pp. (p.6 blank).
    Contents: BWV 933-8 in that order.
    Title: Six Preludes/ (für Anfänger auf dem Clavier) par J.S.
    Bach.
    Hand: J.C. Kittel (1732-1809; pupil of Bach's, 1748-50).

No autograph or early MS copy of the Six Preludes survives: all the
sources listed above date from the 2nd half of the 18th or the 1st
half of the 19th century. However, as far as the notes themselves are
concerned, the text appears to be unproblematic: the sources trans-
mit them uniformly, apart from a few obvious copying errors
which have been corrected in this edition without specific notice.
Ornamentation and phrasing, on the other hand, vary to some
extent from one MS to another. All these markings, regardless of
source, have been reproduced in this edition, for we can be no
more sure in one case than another that they were authorized by
Bach himself. Even ornaments common to all the sources are sometimes doubtful. The combined shake and turn, for example, which
occurs in b.4 of Prelude No.1 and in b.23 of No.3, is a com-
monplace of C.P.E. Bach's keyboard music but somewhat unex-
pected in that of his father.

Still more surprising is the note e^3 (b.46 of Prelude No.4) which
lies outside Bach's normal keyboard compass (see the discussion of
this question in A. Dürr: 'Tastenumfang und Chronologie in
Bachs Klavierwerken', *Festschrift G. von Dadelsen*, Stuttgart,
1978, pp.73 ff.). This, in conjunction with the exceptional ornaments and the late date of the extant sources, raises the possiblity
of unauthorized intervention at some period. In any event, there is
no certainty that the six pieces were collected together to form a set
– still less conceived as such – by Bach himself. The symmetrical
key-scheme in which the pieces are ordered in Sources B, C and E
– C c d D E e – is, on the other hand, fully in line with Bach's habits

(except that he would surely have adopted alternating major and
minor modes; C c D d E e).

In his famous Bach biography (*Über Johann Sebastian Bachs
Leben, Kunst und Kunstwerke*, Leipzig, 1802; quoted here in the
English translation of 1820 which is reprinted in full in H.T. David
and A. Mendel: *The Bach Reader: a Life of Johann Sebastian Bach
in Letters and Documents*, London, 1945; revised ed. 1966) Johann
Nikolaus Forkel gives an interesting description of the origin of the
six pieces, presumably based on information gathered from one of
the Bach sons. After discussing the touch exercises prescribed by
Bach in keyboard lessons, he adds:

> If he found that anyone, after some months of practice, began to
> lose patience, he was so obliging as to write little connected
> pieces, in which those exercises were combined together. Of this
> kind are the six little Preludes for Beginners . . . He wrote them
> down during the hours of teaching and, in doing so, attended
> only to the momentary want of the scholar. But he afterwards
> transformed them into beautiful, expressive little works of art.

No.1 in C, BWV 933.   The alto appoggiatura in b.4 is present in
Source B only.
No.2 in C minor, BWV 934.   Key signature: two flats (A, B, D);
three flats (C, E).
No.3 in D minor, BWV 935.   Rhythm of b.23, R.H. corrected
subsequently in Source B to quaver-crotchet.
No.4 in D, BWV 936.   The shake in b.3 and the slurs in bb.4-6
are from Source E.
No.5 in E, BWV 937.   Shake in b.10 from A & D (B: mordent
instead).
No.6 in E minor, BWV 938.   The ornament in b.9 is an editorial
conjecture based on Source E (✶). The phrasing in bb.11, 13, 15,
22, 24, 41, & 43 is from Source B; that of bb. 12, 14 & 16 from E.

Printed in England by Caligraving Limited Thetford Norfolk   9:00